Sharing Wisdom

Sharing
Wisdom

*The Practical Art
of Giving and
Receiving Mentoring*

Robert J. Wicks

A Crossroad Book

THE CROSSROAD PUBLISHING COMPANY

NEW YORK

The Crossroad Publishing Company
370 Lexington Avenue, New York, NY 10017

Printed in the United States of America

Wicks, Robert J.
Sharing wisdom : the practical art of giving and receiving
mentoring / Robert J. Wicks.
p. cm.
Includes bibliographical references.
ISBN 0-8245-1838-1
1. Interpersonal relations. 2. Mentoring. I. Title.
HM1106.W53   1999
371'.102—dc21   99-38733
CIP

1 2 3 4 5 6 7 8 9 10 04 03 02 01 00

DEDICATION

For the "Quiet Mentors" in life who freely give of their time and wisdom to others and often receive little appreciation in return: parents (especially of adolescents—God bless them!), generous business executives, experienced educators, A.A. sponsors, clergy and nonordained ministers, volunteer helpers, and people who generously reach out to support and guide others.

Thank you.

99497

*The greatest good you can do for
another is not just to share your
riches but to reveal to him his own.*

BENJAMIN DISRAELI

ACKNOWLEDGMENTS

In gratitude to Dr. Gwendolin Herder, President of the Crossroad Publishing Company, for her gentle encouragement and personal guidance of this book through the editorial process. In appreciation, as well, to Bob Byrns, Vice President of Marketing, Sales, and Distribution at Crossroad, who believed in the project from its inception and had incredibly creative ways to reach the diverse audience for which this book is intended—he's amazing! To Janet Stavrou, my assistant at Loyola College, for her feedback on the manuscript while it was in development and for typing numerous drafts until it was "just right." And, last, I offer thanks to my wife and favorite editor–mentor, Michaele. Her thoughtful editing of the manuscript tightened up the prose considerably so readers could relax more with my ideas, stories, and encouragements. But more than that, for her modeling mentoring for me all these years by calling me to acknowledge and accept my true self, to be more gentle and true with others, and to deeply appreciate God's precious gift of life, I'm grateful. What more can one ask of a spouse, friend, and mentor?

Contents

Mentoring— An Invitation to All Adults

~

An Introduction

RECENTLY A COLLEAGUE and I were enjoying a conversation about an article on psychoanalysis published in *The New Yorker*. We both found it intriguing and humorous. But then a surprising thing happened.

After a short pause, in which I could tell he was formulating what he was to say next, my colleague quietly added, "You know, at the end of the article I filled up and cried. When the writer shared his feelings about the death of his analyst, I thought of my own losses. But what I think was most poignant for me was how it reminded me that I had not received the mentoring I needed, or at least desired, in my life.

I'd been in therapy. I'd been supervised on my cases. Yet I felt what I lacked was a wisdom figure, someone with whom to share my hopes, desires, and life in a natural way."

This psychologist's reaction is a common one for many adults today. Because of the shift in family structures and greater mobility in society, mentors are not readily available. Yet most of us deeply feel this need for guidance and encouragement.

For a number of years now I have both received and provided mentoring. At this point I have closed my clinical practice and see only people seeking mentoring. In the process I have discovered that mentoring can and should be provided and received by most adults. Sharing our wisdom and seeking out the insights of others within the framework of ongoing relationships is a time-honored process. Mentoring was a part of our culture in time past. Moreover, many of us probably are now involved in mentoring on an informal basis and don't recognize it.

That we are engaged in such generative relationships, of course, is good. However, the imparting and receiving of wisdom can be greatly enhanced with some basic information and intentionality. That is the reason for the creation of this book.

Sharing Wisdom offers forty brief lessons to make the process of offering and receiving mentoring clearer. The information is designed to be practical and readily usable, and it is intended to help you project your natural talents as well as to better appreciate the wisdom figures in your life. In addition, if at this point you have no mentoring, this book will outline the traits to seek in a person able to fill such a role. Finally, the book ends with answers to common questions on mentoring, a summary list of the mentoring guidelines, and a brief annotated bibliography.

Mentoring, the sharing of wisdom, is a beautiful part of adult life. We see this in the help provided by A.A. sponsors, experienced teachers, business executives, office managers, parents, clergy, and so many other people in both formal and informal relationships. The overall intent of this small volume is to encourage you to enter more deeply into this form of relationship. Not to do so is to miss one of the most rewarding experiences available: the imparting and receiving of life's wisdom.

A Gentle Place

MANY YEARS AGO a colleague I had been mentoring walked into my office, sat across from my desk, stretched out his legs, and announced: "I just finished your latest book, *Availability*, and I really liked it."

"Really?" I responded with a smile.

"Yes, I did." Then, after a few seconds he added, "Too bad you're not like what you've written."

After this had a chance to sink in, I smiled again and said, "Well, of course I'm not like that. Most authors write out of their shadows. They point in directions they believe others-and they themselves-should go. But it sounds as if you're also saying I've let you down in some way. When did this happen?" This question led to a good discussion of the pain and frustration he had felt, not only at my hands but from the actions and attitudes of other faculty members as well.

While no one likes to be told that he doesn't measure up and is a bit of a charlatan, I was glad this colleague felt secure enough in my presence to share his anger, sadness, and sense of alienation. He had been going through a long, tough time and needed a gentle place to open up and let his wounds be seen without fear of further abuse.

When he left I thought of the words of the famous psychologist Alfred Adler: "A neglected child has never known what love and cooperation can be; he makes up an interpretation of life which does not include these friendly forces."

Although the colleague who confronted me did not come from a household marked by neglect, he, like every one of us to some degree, lacked security. It now caused him to doubt that he could trust and depend on any of us for support. Events had eroded his sense of well-being to the point where the belief he had about himself was solely negative. Accordingly, he was struggling to maintain his psychological balance. At this point, because of past hurts, he feared opening up to anyone who did not totally agree with his perception. It was too risky to let anyone in who might cause more suffering. Given all he had been through, this was quite natural. I would have to go very slowly-being supportive without encouraging further problematic behavior that would only cause him more grief.

All of us go through periods when we feel left by ourselves, without "friendly forces" to help us gain perspective and know we are worthwhile, competent, secure, and (maybe most of all) understood. Mentors are not a luxury at such times. We need people we can trust to both love and challenge us to walk through life's dark periods until the darkness opens up new ways to see our lives.

Present darkness caused by a lack of understanding of ourselves can turn into new light for the next phase of our lives. So one of the major undertakings in a mentoring relationship is also primary for those interested in a process of self-understanding and self-appreciation: We need to ensure that we have "safe, friendly forces" in our lives.

Therefore, we must take time to reflect on our friendships. We have to examine whether these forces need to be added to, balanced, or changed. Otherwise, our lives will not be nourished in a way that will help us feel the freedom to relax, simply be ourselves, and learn even when the lessons are difficult to accept. There's an old maxim that still has validity today: If you want to know who someone is, simply find out who her or his friends are. Among those friends we certainly need to include mentors.

MENTORING LESSON 1: *Make your mentoring relationships safe enough for people to share intense feelings.*

The Necessary Ingredient

MENTORS ARE PRIMARILY chosen because of one quality: respect. People offering mentorship are able to foster self-exploration and self-appreciation by the way they treat those who come to them for a listening ear and guidance.

At the end of my time with a very talented business executive, I wanted her to reflect on the progress she had made and to give me an outline of her insights. So I asked, "What do you think has been helpful to you during our time together?"

Instead of the list I anticipated, she focused on one factor: "When I came to see you, I simply watched how you sat with me, and then I began sitting with myself in the same way."

If we find mentors we respect, we will be more apt to listen to their guidance and overcome our resistance to change. So, one of the first ways to identify a mentor is to make a list of people who are truly role models for us. In providing mentorship we have to honestly ask ourselves: Do I respect this person seeking my guidance? If the answer is no, or even a qualified no, then it is best not to offer or agree to provide mentorship. Just as in a marriage, when there is respect practically everything else can be worked out satisfactorily. But if respect is missing, the relationship is sure to falter until this ingredient is found.

MENTORING LESSON 2: *Use respect as the litmus test in seeking or providing mentorship.*

Telling One's Story

ONE OF THE most talented people I know surprised me with how she responded to being asked to be someone's mentor. She said to me, "Could you imagine me being asked to be someone's mentor?" To which I answered, "Yes, I could. What's your hesitation?" She said, "Well, what would I do? I have no idea how to be a mentor."

At that point, knowing her innate wisdom was a real gift to all our friends, I said, "Why don't you meet with her a few times and let her tell you about herself and why she wants to see you at this point in her life?"

She did as I suggested and things went very well, as I knew they would. In initiating the mentoring process, this woman found out that most people don't expect miracles. Also she learned what mentors through the ages have realized: People are greatly relieved when they get a chance to tell their stories to someone who is respectful and attentive.

One fellow I had mentored convinced me to see him late at night, even though I warned him I am not too alert after 9:00 P.M. (Always before I had seen him earlier in the day. During those sessions I felt I had made perceptive comments; I had done helpful things for him.)

When this nighttime visit happened, I was so tired I was practically mute—even the usual Rogerian *ahas* seemed to elude me. After about an hour, when he finished sharing what was on his mind, we drank the last of our herbal tea and I walked him to the door. Just as he was leaving he offered me a final thank-you and, almost as an afterthought added: "You know, I think this was the most profitable time I ever spent with you." That night I learn-ed the true value of listening.

MENTORING LESSON 3: *Offer a receptive listening-space where people can tell their stories.*

4: QUESTIONING

Just a Few Steps from Clarity

I BROKE A tooth. There was no saving it. It had to be pulled.

When I went to the dentist, she spoke about all the possibilities following the extraction. She encouraged me to go through a rather involved process in which I could get a permanent false tooth implanted. I agreed and asked if I would have to walk around with a gap in my mouth until the process was complete. (If I could, I wanted to avoid looking like one of the bad guys in an old Clint Eastwood western.) She indicated that I would be fitted with a flipper (lovely name, eh?), a temporary false tooth attached to a plate that I would put in my mouth each morning and take out in the evening. Overnight, she said, I would have to put it in a glass of water so it wouldn't shrink. There it would sit, reminding me I was toothless and, of course, depressing me.

There was one other insidious problem. While I waited for my gum to heal, the temporary plate that held the false tooth became loose. As a result, a couple of times during public lectures, when I laughed loudly, I almost blew the flipper across the room. Worse yet, sometimes during dinner it got caught in my food, and once I nearly swallowed it. (Please don't dwell on what that might have entailed!)

All in all, the process lasted almost a year. Finally, after having my gums operated on four times without success, I sat in the dentist's office feeling sorry for myself and said, "I give up. Aren't there any alternatives to going on this way?" To which the dentist responded in a surprised voice, "Why yes. We can put in a special type of dental bridge. The whole thing can be completed in just two weeks."

I stared at her wide-eyed and asked, "Well, why didn't you mention this option to me in the first place?"

She simply looked at me and said: "Well, the route you chose really was the best one if it had worked out. But," she added (and I'll never forget these three words), "you never asked." Three important words: *You never asked.*

In today's fast-paced world, abandoning the questioning process before getting a full picture of something or someone is a general failure of communication and understanding others and ourselves. As a matter of fact, it is a common error made by novice therapists and mentors. They don't continue to explore issues because they feel they already have the answer. But by not going on, they short-circuit the discovery process. The same can be said of looking at ourselves.

When we repeatedly encounter cul-de-sacs in our personalities and can't seem to understand why we did or felt something, one of the floors below—the preconscious or unconscious—is where the action is. By questioning ourselves further and relying on good mentors to help us, we can discover more about our unnecessary fears or anxieties and address them directly rather than be unknowingly held hostage by them. But too often we give up too early—possibly because we don't want to exert the effort or see some shortcoming in ourselves. It's easy to avoid proceeding far enough, even when we feel we are looking further.

A friend of mine who is quite outrageous was once in a program designed to help him better understand himself. However, he told me he was resisting self-knowledge and openness without knowing it.

I asked him how he finally realized this. He said that one day the person assigned as his mentor looked at him and said with a twinkle in his eye, "You know, Bill, you are a very deep person...*on the surface.*"

The Buddha once said, "In order to untie the knot, you must first learn how it was tied." When we question ourselves until we get sufficient information to free us from feelings of anxiety, confusion, and self-doubt, we are able to move to new places, where we can glean additional helpful knowledge and direction.

The process of discovery is never-ending; that's what makes life such a mystery and adventure.

MENTORING LESSON 4: *Be sure you don't stop exploring issues too soon; question further, asking for illustrations and clear examples.*

5. MODELING

─◦

Rowing with Muffled Oars

THERE IS A Spanish proverb that boldly warns: "Tell me what you brag about and I'll tell you what you lack."

Quiet action is always preferable to noisy proclamations. Using the metaphor of rowing, all beginners make a great deal of noise paddling around in circles or zigzagging in spurts toward their destination. The contrast is evident when you see an experienced crew team in action. On an early fall morning on the Schuylkill River in Philadelphia, you can see the crew team swiftly cutting through the water like a sharp knife through butter. Their oars dip into the water silently and in unison—it is beautiful to watch.

The same can be said of the well-lived life. One of the goals in the mentoring process is to discover people in different areas of our lives with whom we feel we share personality traits, goals, ethics, and so on, but who seem more self-actualized in ways we would like to be. Once such models are discovered the next step is to emulate them. This is helpful not only when we are unhappy or feel lacking in a particular area but also as a way to further develop talents we already know we have.

To emulate a good model may seem overwhelming unless it is done in small steps. So ask the following question in daily interactions and when facing challenges at work and home: What specific action would my role model take in this situation? Then emulate him or her.

MENTORING LESSON 5: *Encourage people not merely to speak about changing or progressing but to focus on role models who can be emulated in little ways each day.*

6. RESPONSIBILITY

Consequences

THE CHINESE HAVE a wonderful proverb: In nature there are no rewards and punishments—only consequences!

Every action we take has an impact. In mentoring we look at this fact to make it possible to change our style of interaction and decision making. By paying attention to how behavior produces certain results, we can become more responsible, avoid problems, and increase our chances of success. While this sounds simple, we often confuse things by trying to excuse our own behavior and that of others. For instance, a teacher who came to me complained that every time she shared something quite personal with a co-worker, it wound up being spread around the school. I asked, "Knowing this pattern, why do you continue to be vulnerable with him?" She responded, "Oh, he doesn't do it to hurt me. He's a nice guy. It's just that he forgets I told him to keep it to himself."

Remembering the Chinese proverb just quoted, I replied, "Whether someone drops a rock on your head on purpose or by mistake, you still get a bump. If you want to prevent your secrets from making the rounds, stop telling them to this man."

We can make excuses as often and as long as we want—that is our decision. But, we must pay the consequences. It's as simple as that.

MENTORING LESSON 6: *Urge people to take responsibility for their behavior and to become more aware of the consequences of each of their actions.*

~

Lighten Your Heart a Little

ONE OF THE greatest wastes of energy is also one of the biggest obstacles in fostering good interpersonal relations at work and at home. It even disturbs the peace when we are alone. The problem I'm alluding to is: taking oneself too seriously.

We all do it. Even professionals in the healing and helping professions are prone to it. Charles Haddon Spurgeon once said: "Some ministers would make good martyrs. They are so dry, they would burn well!"

We all make mistakes, and that is when we can prevent an unnecessary loss of energy by laughing at ourselves. The executive vice-president of the college where I teach recently resigned after many years of illustrious service. I wanted to send him an E-mail message to express my thanks for his visionary leadership. I thought E-mailing would be quicker than sending him a note on paper.

So I called his office and asked a temporary assistant for the E-mail address. I would have preferred to chat with his secretary, but she had moved on in anticipation of his job change.

The message I composed spoke from my heart and told him things I would only have said face to face. After I sent it off, I returned to the duties of the day. But about five minutes later I was distracted by something on my computer screen. It was a confirmation that my personal message to the vice president had been delivered to every chairperson in the university!

My choice was twofold: either laugh at myself and send another note apologizing for the error or go into the washroom, stick my head in the toilet, and flush repeatedly.

Mistakes and failures are part of full involvement in life. Paradoxically, if we are not failing in life, we are probably not being assertive and creative enough. The more you're involved, the more you fail: case closed.

In mentoring leaders, who must face failure but are very sensitive about the reactions of others, I advise humor, saying, "Next time you fail, picture my scruffy, bearded face over your shoulder saying: 'So many people already think ill of you. What's a few more!' " More seriously, I remind them of the need to share their foibles with a trusted friend who is able to laugh with them at their mistakes.

MENTORING LESSON 7: *When people feel upset over a failure or an onslaught on their image, invite them to laugh at themselves.*

The Parent of Perspective

A WELL-LOVED rabbi was once asked by his people how he could maintain perspective and a sense of satisfaction in such a greedy and needy world. He chuckled and responded, "I have been very, very fortunate in my life. In most instances I only realized I needed something after I already had it."

What the rabbi attributed to "being fortunate" can also be seen as an attitude of deep gratefulness. Yet when gratitude is mentioned, people often respond in two unhelpful ways:

Guilt (The feeling arising from the belief an ethical principle has been violated.): "Oh, I know I should be more grateful given all I have in life."

or *Denial* (Conscious refusal to admit certain reality.):

"It's easy for others to speak about gratefulness. If you knew what *I've* been through, you'd understand."

I consider deep gratefulness a way to ensure that people don't underutilize their gifts because of lack of appreciation. To get around the defensive reactions of guilt and denial, I say to people, "You deserve more in life. And, one of the ways I'm going to help you get it is by helping you to bring to awareness what is *already* positive in your work and home environment as well as in your personality style. We'll use these current gifts to strengthen your hand in life. This will prevent you from feeling needy or weak. So from a stance of health and well-being you can see new gifts."

Gratefulness is indeed the parent of perspective. When you meet people with great attitude, you always find they appreciate all they have—even if at the moment it may appear to outsiders as very little. Moreover, not only do grateful people have perspective, but they attract other healthy people and opportunities. Whereas needy people often put off the very people and possibilities they say they want and need. Gratefulness fosters a positive circle of success; unnecessary neediness produces a negative one.

MENTORING LESSON 8: *Help people foster gratefulness by recognizing the many people and things—including their own talents—that they should appreciate and enjoy.*

Two Words

FOR YEARS I recommended that people seeing me for mentoring find a word for themselves, a name—a description that would truly capture them. I did this because it is important to be able to get in touch quickly with our identity when we are interacting with others. In this way we can share our talents more easily. Moreover, when we face peer pressure, if we know who we are we don't easily lose our sense of self and our value system.

However, when lecturing on this topic recently, I found myself suggesting that those in the audience select two words. After they had selected a word that captures the heart of who they are, I asked them to step into the shadows of their personalities to find a second word. This second word enhances and clarifies the first word so it is better balanced.

For instance, my primary word is *passion*. However, in my book *Living a Gentle, Passionate Life*, I chose *gentle* as the second word. Without that modifier, I sense that instead of being passionate, filled with vitality and an inspiration to others, I would be arrogant and exhibitionist—at the very least intrusive or annoying.

So, both when receiving and when offering mentoring, consider what two words or names would be appropriate for you. This exploration is a fast track to self-knowledge. These words need not be permanent choices. In order for them to accurately reflect who you are, they can and should be periodically reexamined. One way to improve the word selection process is to ask for feedback from people who know you well. Such feedback provides for a comparison between our own self-image and how others see us.

MENTORING LESSON 9: *Ask people to reflect on what one word would best describe them. Then encourage them to find a second word to modify or enhance the first so their presence to others is more balanced.*

10. Nonjudgmental

~

A Little Intrigue

ONE OF THE goals in mentoring is to intrigue people about all of their behavior—especially the aspects that seem to confuse or confound them. Patterns of behavior that people don't like but seem to repeat fit into this category.

Too often such behavior is left untouched because it is unpleasant to look at. Moreover, even when it is viewed, the examination can quickly degrade into: Who's at fault— I or the other person? Such negativity has to be taken out of the consideration if it is to succeed. One way to get people intrigued by all their behavior—even if it is dysfunction-al—is to help them realize that when they project blame, making something the other person's fault, they give away the power to change. Likewise, condemning themselves is counterproductive because learning is diminished when we feel bad about ourselves. I have long felt that behavior we wince at will turn into behavior we wink at.

In a mentoring relationship that is accepting and encouraging, intrigue about how to understand ourselves and gain power increases; the mentoring process gets more and more growthful and open. The goal of clarity then becomes rewarding in itself. And the dangerous myth that if I make a mistake or fail, it is terrible—is debunked.

Both the mentor and person being guided need to get excited about the process in which both failures and successes are nonjudgmentally examined. In this way, both the fear of failure and the desire for approval are replaced by the joy of understanding.

MENTORING LESSON 10: *To cultivate a growthful and open mentoring process, foster intrigue about people's behavior—both successes and failures—and excitement about the process of discovery that leads to clarity.*

Interpersonal Obstacles
to Stand On

His Holiness the Dalai Lama once said, "If you utilize obstacles properly, then they strengthen your courage, and they also give you more intelligence, more wisdom. But if you use them in the wrong way," he added, laughing gently, "you will feel discouraged, failure, depression." One of the most frequent and disturbing such obstacle is a negative interpersonal encounter.

More often than I'd like, I get letters, telephone calls, and visits in which I receive criticism. In some cases it is deserved; in others it may be the result of a misunderstanding. In all cases the comments hurt.

Since there is a cost to me, I have long felt there should also be a benefit. At the very least, humility, at the very best, greater perspective, insight, and resilience.

In mentoring as well as in receiving support and guidance, appreciating the need to see the opportunities in interpersonal obstacles—such as rejection, anger directed at us, sadness others accuse us of causing, or interpersonal tension—is essential.

Different people do this differently. However, here are two helpful aids:

- Experiencing the emotion fully, then letting it move away like water going downhill.
- Not blaming ourselves or condemning others, not personalizing or exaggerating, but instead mining the event to find wisdom where there is worry, and freedom where there is fear. This is possible when we can look at even a negative event dispassionately, putting it in proper perspective. After all, how many upsetting events in the past, even the recent past, are no longer bothersome to us now?

MENTORING LESSON 11: *Show people how to utilize a negative interpersonal encounter by experiencing it fully, then letting their feelings flow away from the experience and, finally, looking at the encounter objectively.*

Put a Sweater On

YEARS AGO ONE of my relatives used to invite me over for pizza and a few soft drinks. Such times together were always enjoyable. We had a lot in common and trusted each other enough to share wishes, plans, successes, and blunders. However, I hated to visit him in the summer because my relative loved air-conditioning. I am sure his unit was a supercharged one with a setting marked "snow." Even after a few hours in his home I was convinced that I left with a thin layer of Freon on my skin.

When I mentioned to a friend how I would sit and freeze in my T-shirt after coming in out of the heat, he laughed and said, "Well, why don't you do something about it?"

"I have," I replied. "I've mentioned it to him jokingly and seriously, to no avail. He either teases me or tells me I'll get acclimatized after a while."

"No," my friend replied. "I didn't mean bringing it to

his attention. I assumed you did that with no results. I just wondered why you didn't take along a sweatshirt or sweater when you visited so you could put it on to keep warm."

Whether we are offering or receiving mentoring, one of the important discernments is determining what power is in our hands, what power isn't. Complaining about something is fine as a first step—it is an expression of how we feel. However, reflecting on what we can do through communication or action to change a situation is clearly a sensible step in taking personal responsibility for improving our lot.

MENTORING LESSON 12: *In every situation help people look carefully for what is within their control.*

⁓

You Don't Have to Be Overwhelmed

YEARS AGO, WHEN I was in my manic phase of doing psychotherapy, I saw patients from early in the morning until late at night. (Thank goodness that stage of life is over!) One day, when a man of about forty called sounding anxious, I just added him at the end of the list of people coming to see me that day. Even though it was 9:00 PM, I wasn't worried, because the priest who referred him usually sent fairly benign cases, with problems that took only a few sessions to resolve.

After I met the man, welcomed him, and jotted down some identifying data, I asked what I could do for him. He responded: "I have an irresistible urge to strangle my wife of ten years." My immediate inner reaction was: "My heavens. With a problem like that you ought to see someone for help!"

Of course, when I calmed down inside, I realized he was indeed seeing someone—*me*. After taking note of my feelings, I utilized them to help me understand both how he felt and what he needed to do to deal with this terrible urge—namely, structure the situation to diminish his sense of being out of control.

So, I responded in a way that I think both recognized his feelings and helped him find relief from their impact: "Feeling this way must be overwhelming to you. Why don't you tell me when these feelings began and what was going on at the time?"

I could see both his face and body relax somewhat. First, he saw that I knew how much pain he was in, so he wasn't alone in it anymore. Second, by asking him to tell me when it *began*, I was implying there would be an end. In addition, I was structuring the problem so that it could be faced in a logical, step-by-step fashion.

In mentoring the problems that come up are usually not as extreme as this example. However, people often do come in somewhat overwhelmed. Our initial reaction may be "They need to see someone wiser and more clinically articulate," and this may be the case. Yet if we follow these four basic steps, a referral may not be necessary.

MENTORING LESSON 13: *When you feel overwhelmed by a story or question put to you, follow these four steps: (1) Take note of your feelings,(2) Tell yourself you don't have to have the one perfect answer or an "instant cure," (3) Let the person know you recognize he or she must be feeling overwhelmed, and (4) Ask questions that allow the problem to be addressed in a manageable, logical way.*

A Caring Presence

LITTLE THINGS CAN make such big differences in people's lives. We often remember later in life small gestures of kindness or rebuff—even ones we know were not intentional.

When I was in high school, there was a girl I thought was wonderful. She saw me as a friend, and I resigned myself to that status even though I wanted to be her boyfriend. Just being with her was fun.

One day when we were to take a walk and have a Coke, I put on my favorite shirt, combed my hair four times, and ran off to meet her. Although she was usually quite prompt, this time she was late. Also, when she came out she was wearing an old jacket, and her hair, rather than being carefully groomed as it seemingly always was, was all askew. I was crestfallen. Not only didn't she look beautiful, but I took it personally. I felt she cared too little for me even as a friend to comb her hair.

In mentoring the same thing can occur. I'll often tell teachers who are in mentoring to appreciate how busy their principals are so if a session begins late or is missed once in a while, or if the principals forget something the teachers have shared, they can remember that it's not meant as a personal affront.

I caution principals or senior teachers to show they value those they are mentoring by being prompt, attentive, and responsive. They may not see the mentoring process as important—after all, this task is often added on to their already full schedule. However, mentoring—as this book is meant to convey—is one of the most significant ways to increase the ripples of one's own wisdom.

MENTORING LESSON 14: *Show that you value your relationships with those you are mentoring in little ways, such as being prompt, attentive, and responsive about what they are sharing and how they are progressing.*

15 · DETACHMENT

~

You Have to Let
Go of the Fish

PROFOUND LESSONS IN life can come to us in even
the silliest of ways if we are open and have others with
whom to share them.

Early one Saturday morning I was drinking coffee,
looking out the back window while I was chatting with my
oldest brother on the portable phone. Suddenly I burst out:
"Wow! Look at that!" My brother said: "Bob, I don't have
a video phone. What is it?"

Instead of responding to him, I yelled to my wife:
"Michaele, quick, come here or you're going to miss this."
As she ran in, she exclaimed, "I want to get a closer look."
To which I responded: "Don't scare it."

Finally, I remembered my brother and said: "You're not
going to believe this. There's a great blue heron in the

yard. Let me see what he's going to do, and I'll call you back."

My wife observed: "I think he's stalking something in the bushes." At that point he stepped into my pond and in quick succession ate four of my prized eight-inch coys.

I was stunned, and when I finally regained speech, I said: "I'm going to defeather that poacher!" To which my wife calmly responded: "If you want the blue heron, you have to let go of the fish."

After letting her know that such statements were grounds for an immediate divorce in Nevada, I laughed and said: "You know, you're right.

Being able to enjoy a new thing often means letting go of something else—even something we really liked. In supporting people to become clear about what they want, we may have to help them see that they might have to let go of something else that may be equally desirable. Detachment from one good thing may not be easy because there is a cost in giving up something that has value for us. Yet, without this ability to move away and let go, one will never realize the reward of new, possibly greater, good choices in life.

MENTORING LESSON 15: *In supporting people to become clear about what they want, help them see that they might have to let go of something else that may be equally desirable.*

16. HOPE

Out of a Dark Hallway

ONCE AFTER MENTORING a troubled doctoral student, I felt a bit down myself. So, I went to an older colleague and shared the experience. When I was done he said: "You really promised that man a great deal. How are you going to deliver?"

"I have no idea."

"Then why did you promise so much?" he asked.

"Because I wanted him to feel better."

At this point he smiled and said: "No wonder you feel depressed!"

After I leaned back in my chair and sighed, he added: "Look, most people who find themselves in difficult circumstances—especially because of their interpersonal styles, like this fellow—get there over time. These things don't occur overnight, and they won't be solved overnight. The hope you give as a mentor is in sitting with people in the darkness with the belief that together you can begin to find a way out."

This lesson has stuck with me. I have realized more and more that quick fixes are not the answer, even though we would like magic. However, most people do feel better when someone calmly sits with them, in empathy, and begins the process of looking at alternatives and potential remedies.

I now tell people who are seeing everything negatively that when someone is in a dark hallway, he may imagine the rest of the house as without light. But when he opens a door to new possibilities, then he may see the truth: that there is light in the rest of the house after all.

Some are still discouraged and say: "But I've behaved this way my whole life. What hope is there for change?"

Using another image, I add: "If you were lost in a forest for days, you might never find a way out. However, if you can get to a clearing on top of a hill and see a way out—even though it may take a long time to follow it, the natural feeling is relief. It doesn't matter how many steps you've taken into a forest, when you finally take a correct step out, it feels wonderful. The same can be said about the journeys in our personal and professional lives."

MENTORING LESSON 16: *Recognize that some problems have developed over years. Don't be discouraged by this, but let it encourage hope, patience and an appreciation of step-by-step solutions.*

~

Passionate and Practical

THE SPIRIT OF the mentoring process can best be described by two words: passionate and practical. As a mentor you must be fully yourself, a passionate, practical presence to others.

By *passionate* I don't mean exuberant or exhilarating, although in some cases that may be true. What I mean is that the person seeking guidance should feel the mentor's sense of life, his or her commitment to excellence and compassion, his or her honesty and transparency.

If we look at any person in history who has impressed us, we will see first and foremost a passionate presentation of his or her own personality. If we were put in a room with people of diverse personalities such as Mohandas Gandhi, Abraham Lincoln, Eleanor Roosevelt, Joan of Arc, and Aristotle, we would probably change;

their extra*ordinary* personalities would have an impact on us.

The same is possible for us if we are self-aware, transparent, and committed with all our hearts to both wisdom and relationship. By being with us, people can borrow from our sense of self and be moved to delve deeply into themselves so they, too, can express themselves fully.

The mentoring encounter should also be *practical*. People should feel they were heard, understood, helped to gain clarity, and given feedback based on our experience. This does not mean that we must come up with answers; in many cases that is not possible. But a willingness to hear out the challenges being faced, to exert the effort to give as much clarity as possible about the situation, and to share our own wisdom and experience is important.

MENTORING LESSON 17: *Be fully yourself (a passionate presence), and be practical, listen carefully, help seek greater clarity, and share your own wisdom and experience.*

Your Quiet Little Place in the Garden

YEARS AGO I WAS intrigued by a U.S. senator who said that the greatest challenge facing the Congress is not enough time to think. I feel this is a truth for most of us today.

When people have covered a good deal of ground in a mentoring session or we seem at an impasse, I suggest reflection. "Do you take bubble baths?" I ask (usually much to their surprise). Whether or not they say yes, I suggest they take our conversation and sit with it in a relaxed way to see what comes to mind so we can discuss it the next time we get together. We need to encourage people to spend time daily in silence and solitude, even if it's only two or three minutes, to integrate the lessons of mentoring and of life.

We miss so much because we don't give ourselves

time in silence and solitude. Such time offers us a chance to reflect, let the alternatives rise to the surface, and get some distance from the type of thinking that occurs under pressure.

A favorite garden plaque of mine says: "There's always music amongst the trees in the garden, but your heart must be quiet to hear it." Too often we resist taking time to listen to this music because the only "music" we hear in quiet moments is played to the tune of our worries.

When we slow down, often we are barraged with the worries of the day. However, the best approach to dissipating worries which are obstacles to our being drawn to this necessary reflective process is to look them right in the face. Although initially this will not seem to help, sticking with this discipline will usually lessen the intensity of the preoccupations. Worries wear themselves out, especially when we are in a relaxed place.

Another reason we avoid silence and solitude is that when we quiet down things we have denied or avoided that lay just below the surface may show their heads. This is to be expected. Nature abhors a vacuum so when we leave our conscious life empty, the preconscious rises into this space and confronts us with our lies, boredom, charlatanism, failures, and fears. However, if we don't run away or give them too much credence, they can be our teachers. They can give us information about what we tend to be anxious about, believe, or value. By stepping into this "shadow" with intrigue rather than fear, with a desire to appreciate all of ourselves (instead of a desire to make ourselves up the way we feel we should be), we can have even greater knowledge—knowledge that can help us to be free from the unknown.

MENTORING LESSON 18: *Encourage people to spend time daily in silence and solitude—even if it's only two or three minutes—to integrate the lessons of mentoring and of life.*

Do You Want These Rules?

ONE OF THE great awakenings that mentoring provides is an awareness that we have hidden rules in life. We follow them without knowing we are doing it. We let them guide us even when they no longer make sense.

Our rules may have started as good ideas. They could be the stated or assumed values of our parents, church, business, or society. More often than not, however, there are at least four problems with them:

1. They are distorted versions of what we believe we have been taught or have learned.

2. They have been assimilated without critique or reflection—possibly because we embraced them when we were very young or impressionable.

3. They have taken on the gravity of the Ten Commandments—even though we were the ones who incorporated them into our belief system.

4. They may be unconsciously guiding us in the very direction we do not want to go and consciously say we are against.

You can bring to the surface and examine such rules quite easily. First, note when you feel strong emotions or convictions. Then ask yourself these seemingly naive questions: Why am I feeling this way? and On what stone is it written that what I believe about this is true?

For instance, once when working with someone who had a very full schedule, I noticed she seemed unusually upset when she was able to do only an acceptable job. Everything had to be perfect. On top of this, she felt she could not turn down any assignments. A volatile combination—perfectionism and no limits to tasks accepted—are a sure recipe for chronic stress leading to burnout.

My response was to question her rules. "You say you feel all is lost if you don't do a perfect job on any task you are assigned. I wonder on what stone that commandment is carved. Also, you can't refuse any assignment. No is not an acceptable word. By this are you saying that if you are capable of getting an A on ten tasks, then it is humanly possible to get the same grade if you have twenty, thirty, or forty tasks with no additional resources?"

When she saw how her rules would eventually defeat her, produce a rageful outburst, or lead to sickness (one way an extreme conscience gives us a vacation), this woman recognized that old, unquestioned premises were tyrannizing her and needed to be examined and changed if she were to thrive in freedom.

MENTORING LESSON 19: *Help people bring to the surface, examine, and discard hidden rules that limit their freedom and are no longer relevant to their lives.*

~

Education, Not Training

ONE OF MY FAVORITE Jewish proverbs is this: *"Do not limit your children to your own learning, for they have been born in another age."*

Mentoring succeeds when we share our experience and wisdom with others, in other words, when we convey approaches we have used to solve problems. Yet the ultimate goal is to encourage others to develop their *own* ways of making sense of the challenges that face them.

The mentoring process goes awry when, rather than educating people to use their own talents in the new situations they encounter, we seek to train them, like animals, to follow our lead. Without the freshness of freedom and collaboration, people in mentoring won't learning to solve problems by themselves, make their own decisions, or develop plans to break new ground.

If someone comes to me, says he has just been fired as manager of a brush factory, and wants help to find a new brush factory manager's job, I can give him feedback that will wake him up. For instance, I can show him that by seeing himself as a manager, he can look for *any* job that requires leadership experience—not just jobs in brush factories. I can also urge him to find a "headhunter" to help in his job search or encourage him to seek career guidance. However, only to let him know how I searched for my past jobs and to persuade him to do the same would accomplish very little.

MENTORING LESSON 20: *Use your experience to help educate people in ways of approaching life differently. Offer them fresh information and advice that will be helpful in their particular, unique situations.*

21. Steps

A Logical Way

ONE OF THE wonderful events in mentoring happens when chaos meets calm problem-solving. Often people come with emotionally laden issues. They are angry, sad, hurt, or exuberant, and because of this feel a bit lost, confined, or adrift—even strong positive emotions can create these feelings of disorientation.

As mentors we often feel people's emotions sweep over us like a cold wave or a blast of hot air. The next thing we may feel is the upset or panic that comes from thinking: "She's going to want me to help her make sense of this and become grounded. How will I ever do that?"

After feeling both the impact of people's emotions and our own insecurity about living up to the task, we need to let them tell their story in detail so we can relax with it, and then help them see the five steps in problem solving without having the unrealistic expectation that things can be totally changed overnight:

1. *Ventilation:* Recognize and describe what happened in detail.
2. *Diagnosis:* Determine the source or sources of these feelings.
3. *Planning:* Decide what to do.
4. *Intervention:* Do what can be done.
5. *Letting go!* Know what can be controlled and don't waste energy on what can't.

By following these steps, people will reach greater clarity; feel more in control and clear about what happened, why it occurred, and what they can do about it; and gain a sense of satisfaction from the actions they take (whether they succeed or not) because they will know they did what they could.

MENTORING LESSON 21: *After experiencing someone's strong emotions, take a step back and offer this logical problem-solving approach: ventilation, diagnosis, planning, intervention, and letting go.*

⌒

Scream, Understand... Then Let Go!

EMOTIONS ARE WAKE-UP calls. They need to be fully felt so we can appreciate what is going on in our lives or, more aptly, in our minds (since all emotions result from our interpretation of events). In addition, ignoring or forgetting our emotional events is tantamount to not paying attention to a smoke or auto alarm, risking that our future will go up in flames or be stolen from us because we didn't respond.

However, once we wake up, the alarm is no longer important. Action is! This is especially the case with respect to anger.

I often tell people that if they grab a hot poker, screaming loudly is natural. However, after they wake themselves up to the situation with a scream, they should understand what is causing them pain and let go of the poker—not continue to hold on to the poker screaming.

Three elements are essential to face an unpleasant situation: Fully experience the emotion, understand the cause and impact, and let go. The "letting go" process, though, is not easy in most situations. And so, although it is obviously incorrect grammatically, to emphasize the patience needed, I prefer to refer to it as "letting go-*ing*."

Letting go is an *ongoing* process in which the event is never completely let go of. At some level it is always remembered and has emotion attached to it. However, when the process of letting go is successful, the event that triggered so much emotion takes a different, less potent, actually instructive place in our lives.

Unfortunately, when we encounter difficult situations, we often set them aside or are frozen by them. The common initial responses to unpleasant events are anger, bitterness, hardness, intellectualization (superficial thinking that prevents real emotional experiencing), and depression. If these emotions are not judged but used to encourage looking directly at the event with a hope of understanding and growing from it, then depth and compassion become possible.

Therefore, standing with people to patiently explore something is essential. In some cases, when the event is beyond the scope of mentoring (severe trauma for instance) referral to a mental health professional is a good idea. However, this does not mean abandoning the mentoring process, which can be a consistent source of much-needed additional support.

MENTORING LESSON 22: *Help people turn negative experiences into life lessons by experiencing them fully, understanding them completely, and letting them go.*

23. PATIENCE

Worth the Wait

ONE OF THE primary gifts of mentoring is modeling the value of patience. In the United States, one of the general norms is to react—and to react quickly if possible. The value of patience has been all but forgotten. In the stock market people look for instant results; long-term value is often virtually neglected. In literature the weighty volume with wonderfully developed characters is passe while novelettes that offer immediate emotional gratification sell by the truckload. The same mentality can infect a school, business, religious organization, or family. The thinking is: If an interpersonal difficulty arises, react immediately before it gets worse!

Yet reacting soon after something happens can actually make things worse. In chairing meetings or leading my department, I find that when I have patience most problems work themselves out. Even those that don't usually need less intervention once tempers have cooled and people have had a chance to involve themselves informally in the process. In reality, there are very few real emergencies that need immediate action.

A mentor's experience in this regard will be helpful in preventing people who seek guidance from moving too quickly. Also, once people see how valuable patience is, they will begin to experiment with it instead of reacting with knee-jerk responses.

Patience with difficult people is also essential. Some people seem so trying and unappreciative. One way to deal with such difficulty is to focus on the process of relating to them and not on the results. In other words, if you are able to be clear, welcoming, and not frightened off or crushed by others' anger or chronic disappointment, you should see this ability as a victory of sorts.

Also, I have long advocated low expectations and high hopes, especially when relating to people who are difficult, rigid, or self-righteous. By this I mean that I try not to set goals for people to meet but instead to be open to seeing movement in ways I didn't expect. In this way I am less often disappointed and also able to take stock of and reinforce progress in an array of areas I might have missed if I had focused on a narrow set of goals.

MENTORING LESSON 23: *Model and teach patience as a way to let people and systems heal themselves. When dealing with difficult people, have low expectations and high hopes.*

Positive Contamination

MENTORING GIVES PEOPLE a chance to encounter someone who has thrived on life. This does not mean that the mentor didn't have pain, experience shame, make mistakes—even big ones. But mentors are people who didn't settle in life. They lived it and continue to do so, even though in society's eyes they may not seem successful or relevant anymore.

Mentors are infectious. They model fresh, frank, and innovative ways to live life. To do this they need not be brilliant, famous, wealthy, good looking, or accomplished. They simply need to be enthusiastic and genuinely themselves, and to see life as precious. Who they are provides as much to the people seeking mentoring as what they know.

To be this way mentors need only take time each day to reflect or meditate on the gift of life and to embrace fully who they are with as much confidence as they can. Then, as they greet the day and its mentoring opportunities, their attitude will instill confidence and encourage people to borrow from their passion for life. They will be providing positive contamination.

MENTORING LESSON 24: *Value who you are as an ordinary person and see life as truly precious; then your passionate, courageous attitude will be positively infectious.*

~

New Knowledge
for the Mentor

Henry David Thoreau once said: "If you see someone coming to do good for you, run for your life!" In theory it's great to hear prophetic words calling us to wake up and see an unpleasant aspect of ourselves. Yet when a spouse, child, friend, or co-worker shows us something about ourselves that we had consciously or unconsciously kept hidden, it's a different story. This is also the case with people who come to us for mentoring.

Once a person who was seeing me as a therapist came into my office and stretched out full length on the sofa. (Since I'm not an analyst, I recognized something was awry!) Before I could say anything, she said: "I always speak in the sessions. This time you do the talking." Then she closed her eyes and folded her arms across her chest.

It didn't take a psychologist to see she was annoyed with me. So I asked why she was upset. At that point she shared the reason for her anger. Her emotions seemed out of line with the event she recounted to me, and I told her so. I believed that it was important for her to see this so she would not blow things out of proportion in situations that were less secure than her therapist's office.

When I said this she sat up, looked me in the eyes, and declared: "Look, as a woman it has taken me a long time to reach the point where I felt secure and free enough to both feel and express my anger. So if you have a problem with my being angry, I suggest you get over it, because I'm not going to let go of it until I'm ready."

Her words hit me with such a truthful force that I laughed out loud. She was right on the money. It wasn't that her anger was out of place. My discomfort with other people's anger was the real issue. This interaction was therapeutic for me as well as for my client because it clearly emphasized that I needed to be acutely aware of my own feelings lest they become obstacles in the mentoring or therapy session.

When we talked further about the incident, not only was she affirmed in her position but she was also able to see me model a humble way of dealing with new information about myself that is not very nice on the surface, but underneath is very helpful to know.

MENTORING LESSON 25: *Be attuned to your feelings so you can recognize when your own denials, repressions, or interpersonal games come to light in a mentoring interaction. And model being open to helpful, albeit unpleasant insights.*

26. Little Jolt

A Sailor's Pants

ONCE WHEN MY daughter was in a foul mood, I did what parents of moody teenagers the world over would love to do when every effort at cheering them up fails: I ran away! Well, not far actually. I went to check the mailbox.

When I saw the flag down on the box, I knew the notes I had left for the letter carrier were gone. So I hoped that something good might be there for me (or better yet, for my daughter!). As it turned out, there was a letter from one of my publishers on a new book idea. The suggestion so fascinated me that I read it while walking slowly back up to the house.

I was so absorbed by the letter that I didn't realize I had veered off a bit, and I walked straight into a tree, fell back, and dropped the mail. Not really hurt but feeling foolish, I got up, retrieved the mail, looked around to see if anyone had noticed, then walked on to the house, this time watching where I was going.

Just as I got in the door I saw my daughter doubled over with laughter, tears streaming down her face. Obviously, she'd seen me walk into the tree. So I said: "Oh, and I suppose if I'd knocked myself out, it would have made you happy for a month!" To which she laughed even louder. One slapstick event can be just the little jolt needed to change our moods. Little things can lighten our dark skies. And we as mentors must remember this.

After a storm, as the clouds started to break up a little, my mother would often look up and say to me, "Oh, there's enough blue in that sky now to make a sailor's pants. Soon it's going to be a sunny day again."

One of the challenges in mentoring is not to be captured by the sometimes dark, limited frame of reference of the people coming to see us. Instead, look for the beginning of a possibility or the little jolt that will help people to see that a new perspective, additional learning, or a hitherto missed possibility is present. This is not so much a lesson in positive thinking as a commitment not to be captured by negative beliefs. One of the best ways to identify the presence of the new is to look for measures of success or payoffs other than the ones a person is staring at.

Even in dire situations this is important to remember. When people are encountering a major loss, they may be more compassionate to other family members than they have ever been. When they have failed in a goal at work, they may recognize they have much to learn in leadership or collaborative skills. Sometimes good knowledge—even wisdom—can break through only when we fail or confront darkness. Mentors must be attuned to this fact to help people integrate such learning into their way of viewing the world rather than let it be just a fleeting insight.

MENTORING LESSON 26: *Notice the essential learning that is present in all failures and losses so it can be integrated into the people's wisdom. Sometimes infusing a little jolt of humor or hope is all that's needed to break the bonds of negativity.*

27. THE FRUITS

~

What's the Difference?

AT SOME POINT in the mentoring relationship religious people will often share what they feel are breakthrough events in the development of their faith. A
Buddhist may speak about a *kensho* (epiphany) experience
during *zazen* (sitting meditation), a Hindu may describe
what the Upanishads refer to as "a turning around in the
seat of one's consciousness," a Christian coming back from
Medjugorie in Yugoslavia may report a miraculous event
involving Jesus' mother, Mary, or a Jew who finally had an
opportunity to pray at the Wailing Wall may describe having been deeply moved.

All these are beautiful, life-giving experiences, which
merit hearing and sharing. Significant occurrences are filled
with meaning that may shape how people live the rest of
their lives. But, unfortunately, this is not always the case.

As a result, whenever someone tells me about some spiritual or psychological breakthrough, after the person has had a chance to relish the experience with me, I ask the famous biblical question "What are the fruits of this experience?"

A wonderful insight, a feeling of oneness with the world, a spiritual solace, a clarity of mind can be a remarkable event to be nostalgic about. However, it can also have lasting ripples in how we see the world and interact with others.

When we as mentors question people about possible deeper effects, they may get defensive. This is a sign to step back, but the seed has been planted. The initial question, while causing some unpleasantness, has nudged people to look—as much as their defensiveness will allow—at the true impact of their religious experience.

Often, however, people respond with a great deal of interest to the question, especially when it is begun with a recognition of the profundity of the experience. For instance, "From what you have just told me, not only in words but by the tone of your voice and the look on your face, this event was truly an epiphany, an awakening. Whew! Even hearing you tell it affects me [say this only if it is true—which it often is for me]. I am sure it really struck you as amazing. How has it changed you over time in the way you both see and live your life?"

By asking such questions you can really help people's inner experiences connect with how they live with others.

My sense is a genuine religious epiphany, psychological experience, or spiritual awakening is not worth much—or perhaps is not significant at all—if it doesn't result in greater service, compassion, and generosity of spirit.

MENTORING LESSON 27: *When people relate profound spiritual or psychological experiences, help them explore the fruits of these events.*

28. DISTANCE

Don't Catch the Disease

THERE IS A Zen saying that life is like stepping into a boat that is about to go out to sea and sink. Although on first blush this sounds morbid, it's true, isn't it? Life isn't permanent. Time passes quickly and we die. So, we need to appreciate the preciousness of life and share that attitude with those we mentor.

The greatest enemies of this appreciation of the fleeting nature of life and the preciousness of the now are those factors that encourage loss of perspective. Among them is the self-inflicted misery of people around us at work and in our families. Therefore, we need to cultivate some distance so we don't catch their psychological and spiritual disease, their proneness to misery. We can do this through meditation in the morning. With just a few minutes of quiet in solitude, wrapped in gratitude, facing our own limitedness in life (that's a nice way of saying mortality), we can center ourselves on what is really important so we won't be caught up in other people's loss of perspective.

Sometimes the people we mentor are moody and preoccupied. Instead of self-awareness and gratefulness for the guidance they are receiving, they are busy blaming the world (including us) and exaggerating their own lacks, faults, and misfortunes. To expect them to behave otherwise is only to invite frustration and get pulled into the misery ourselves. But to keep our center and hope that somehow they can find serenity from contact with our peace is a good goal. Also, to avoid personalizing the pain they direct toward us is a sure way not to give away our perspective.

When begging for help for the girls in her school during a local famine, Mother Teresa was spit at by a man angry that she had approached. She said, "Well, that's for me. Now what do you have for my girls?" This very man became one of her lifelong friends and supporters.

Humor also helps us keep a sense of distance. In M*A*S*H, a TV series based on experiences in a field hospital in Korea during the war, humor was a centerpiece of the characters' unstated psychological strategy to maintain sanity and perspective. If we lack a sense of humor, surrounding ourselves with good-humored people is a must. Even watching shows or movies or reading books that help us laugh is good medicine.

There is a wisdom saying from the abbas and ammas of

the fourth-century northern Persian desert that states: "If you see someone sinking in quicksand, don't reach out a hand. Instead grab a stick and reach out lest you both go down in the process." That stick is also a metaphor for the right degree of psychological and spiritual distance.

MENTORING LESSON 28: *Maintain a reasonable distance from the negativity of others and maintain perspective through morning meditation focused on the preciousness and brevity of life. Also keep a sense of humor handy to break the negative projections people try to place on you.*

It's Your Responsibility...
So Don't Be Surprised

IN FORMAL MENTORING (parent-child, clergy-parishioner, supervisor-supervisee, A.A. sponsor–A.A. member) boundaries are a must. Moreover, keeping them is the responsibility of the mentor.

I once asked a more experienced colleague how he maintained boundaries when someone he was helping became enamored with him. He offered a simple formula: "I simply acknowledge the positive comments. I indicate that it's natural for people to have such feelings for someone who is journeying with them and sharing intimate, challenging stories and fears. But, not too worry, because I will keep the boundaries for the two of us. And I do. I do."

People appreciate boundaries because boundaries allow the freedom to express intense positive and negative feelings without worrying that they will be acted upon. The danger comes when the mentor forgets to maintain boundaries or is not alert to their possible violation. "I was surprised by it, and therefore the situation got out of hand before I knew what happened" is no excuse.

Informal mentoring between acquaintances or friends is another story. Some of these relationships develop into something more and end in very happy marriages. In other cases disaster results. Being attuned to the possibility of such changes in feeling and talking about them is the best way to handle such potential shifts.

MENTORING LESSON 29: *Accept your responsibility for maintaining boundaries. Being surprised is no excuse.*

30. Withdrawing Projections

Annoying Reminders

In the mid-1980s the shortcomings of two of my acquaintances caused a breakthrough for me. I keep this memory in mind as I sit down in meditation each day, and I share it at some point with all the people I mentor. If they get the point of the story and reflect on it daily, life will change for them. It is as powerful as that.

The first acquaintance was a wonderfully helpful woman in her thirties. She had a heart of gold. The problem was she was very rigid, detail-oriented to the point of exasperation, frightened of being alone, and tended to see things in black and white. This last difficulty could result in rage when she perceived an injustice. It rarely occurred to her to give the person in power the benefit of the doubt. In fact, she gave little or no attention or care to other people's problems.

I felt stressed around her, especially when she was

seesawing between negative extremes. On the one hand, if no one at the hospital where she worked involved her in meetings or projects, she felt unloved, unwanted. On the other, if she was asked to help, she would get overwhelmed, become short-tempered, and feel insecure when her behavior brought retaliation. This, in turn, led to more anger and a great deal of self-doubt and rumination.

Normally I would just let her behavior wash over me, but on one occasion it was different because another acquaintance was going through changes. This person's Achilles' heel was security. Although forty-one years old, he was constantly preoccupied with his retirement. This was before the advent of the Internet, so he couldn't log on any time to find out how his stock portfolio was doing, but he did check the newspaper each morning. Also, he was constantly planning where he would live. With seven children in five states, he would change venues for his later years as often as the weather would change.

Usually his antics wouldn't bother me either. This irritating behavior aside, he was a dear fellow with whom I enjoyed working. However, on this occasion he was particularly upset, and even my usual teasing didn't snap him out of it. Then the woman I just described called from the hospital to let me know how she felt I had been insensitive to her the last time we were together.

The whole business rattled me so, I brought it to the

self-debriefing I do each evening to quiet myself before bedtime. As I sat there gently reviewing my day, I thought about these two people, and the Zen saying I shared in Lesson 28 came to mind again: Life is like stepping into a boat that is about to go out to sea and sink. And I thought: Don't these two people know how precious and fragile life is? Since today may be their last day on this earth, why would they give away their perspective on such little things and not enjoy the beautiful life they both have?

Then it hit me like a bolt of lightning: Why am I doing the same thing? Why am I letting their annoying behavior take away my joy, my appreciation of the precious now?

I had been projecting blame onto them just as they were projecting blame onto other situations and people. I needed to withdraw my projections and enjoy the wonder of my life now. I don't mean I needed to blame myself for being foolish. That would do nothing—just as picking on these two misguided individuals wouldn't aid them. However, I did need to learn from these situations.

So, in a healthy and practical sense, withdrawing projections means to me that: every time I get annoyed at someone for losing perspective and forgetting the preciousness of life (as I surely will again and again), I need to see my annoyance as a wonderful red flag to wake me up to the reality that I have lost perspective. I need to remind myself immediately that my life is too short and wonderful to get lost in their darkness. And such red flags also call me back to the necessity of centering myself quietly in my morning meditation and my evening debriefing so this happens less and less.

MENTORING LESSON 30: *Remind yourself and others to use the red flag of annoyance to see the need to withdraw projections and let peace, composure, and gratitude return.*

31. Self-Debriefing

Evening Catharsis

WHEN I WAS young, my father used to come home from work during the holidays, open the front door, throw his hat on the table, and ask: "Who's sick?" Chances were one of us would be down with the flu, chicken pox, the measles, a virus, or something else. It never failed! The holidays always had one of us laid up sick. From a psychological perspective, the same thing occurs in school faculties, business departments, or any other regularly assembled group. Family systems theory teaches us that at any given time some one will be acting up. The question is not whether it will happen, but who it will be.

Irritating, anxiety-producing, and energy-draining encounters need to be recognized as quickly as possible so we can psychologically and spiritually "right ourselves." We need to be jolted to see how easy it is to lose perspective and become enmeshed in trivialities by personalizing someone else's lack of balance. However, in addition to doing this on the spot, we also should try to deal with such events during an evening catharsis.

Each evening I suggest people take just five or ten minutes to breathe with the day until the residue is gone. Find a quiet room or corner, light a candle if you wish, and sit down. Keep your back straight, your hands on your lap, your eyes slightly open or closed, and breathe in a relaxed fashion.

After your body eases and relaxes, reflect on how precious, wonderful, and lucky you are to have been born. If negative life events come to mind, smile and say to yourself: "Yes, that happened, but so did so much love in quiet little ways befall me and the wonderful people I've met."

If you find it difficult to relax, just spend the five minutes or more relaxing. That will be enough for today. If you can ease up, then review the day nonjudgmentally to see what you can learn. If you find your are getting angry at yourself, be more gentle: You did your best. If you see yourself getting upset at others, appreciate their ignorance. You don't have to forgive them yet, but at least recognize they are ignorant. If they weren't, they or you wouldn't have behaved that way. So don't pick on yourself, and don't waste negative energy on others—but, as when watching a docudrama, learn so you can interact more clearly and strongly next time.

Once the time is up, recognize that you have done

what you can for one day. If you wake up during the night and start ruminating, repeat again: "I've done what I can for now. Morning will offer new chances." Then think of loving people and events in your life as you rest lightly.

Sound impossible? Not really. With practice self-debriefing every evening will help settle you and help you mentor others to get closure in the same way.

MENTORING LESSON 31: *Take a few minutes in silence and solitude each evening to review your day nonjudgmentally so you can get closure and learn how to help others do the same.*

Helpful Comments

Mentors often express this concern: "I worry about whether I will say just the right thing to help people." This reaction among A.A. sponsors, parents of adolescents, business executives, teachers, clergy, and others is based on the erroneous belief that there is one magical answer.

Once when a supervisor told me a young person with whom he was doing therapy got angry and picked up a heavy paperweight to throw at him, I waited in great expectation to hear what he would say next. My fantasy was he had made a comment that melted both the paperweight and the patient's anger.

When he didn't respond in a few seconds, I said: "Well, what did you do?" He smiled and calmly replied: "I got up and ran out of the room!"

The perfect statement doesn't exist. What do exist

though are helpful comments—one of which may strike home and eventually be embraced by the person we are mentoring. All we can do is offer our presence and comments and let the outcome rest lightly.

When people share a concern with me, I simply let them tell me all about it. Just sharing feelings is good medicine. Then we explore what they did about it and how effective these actions were. I also ask what else they plan to do.

As I listen to all of this and review the possibly inappropriate interpretation they are giving to events (for example, "I really am a failure as a person because I didn't succeed in this instance"), I seek as much clarity as I can obtain.

Then I offer as many helpful responses as I can. It is up to the people themselves to select what fits with their unique situation. Frequently a person will tell me in retrospect, "The one thing you said to me last time that really made sense was ___." Sometimes, the statement that was most helpful I don't even remember saying. Whereas, what I felt were the "really insightful comments" made no impact.

MENTORING LESSON 32: *Once you have listened to the individual's concerns, explore what he or she did and how effective it was, seek as much clarity as possible, offer as many helpful responses as you can, then let the outcome rest lightly.*

Being an "Adult"

In the 1960s and 1970s transactional analysis was much in vogue. *I'm OK, You're OK, Games People Play,* and *Born to Win* are just three of the better-known books published on this method of treatment and self-awareness.

This approach translated some of the concepts of traditional therapy into popular jargon. One such relabeling changed *superego, ego,* and *id* to the labels *parent, adult,* and *child.* Put simply, practitioners of TA hoped people would see when they or others were behaving like a parent (punitive, pedantic) or a child (regressive, impulsive) so they could seek to move toward the more responsible, healthy behavior of an adult.

One of the goals in mentoring is to recognize when we or others are behaving as children or parents. This is important so we don't get hooked into behaving as either children or parents ourselves.

When a person acts like a child, we may get hooked into becoming childish as well or into moving to a dominant parent position. Similarly, when a person comes across as a parent, we may be tempted to respond by being another parent and fighting for control or by being a child who is either dependent and submissive or rageful and rebellious.

Indications that one is moving from a healthy, assertive adult position to one that's either childish or demeaning are the presence of negative emotions such as rage and resentment, although other strong emotional responses also are tips that we are no longer feeling clear and calm. Helping people pick up these cues is a way of aiding them to get "unhooked" much earlier.

As mentors we also need to be alert to our own tendencies to get hooked. Once, when I pointed out to a feeling-controlled individual that he seemed angry, he replied: "I am not!" While my temptation was to fall into a child's position by insisting ("You are too. You are too!") or a parental one by intellectualizing (a long-winded explanation using psychological terms to explain why he was resisting my interpretation) or to be pedantic ("Why, just look at your red face; it's obvious you're angry"), I was able to check these urges. Then, as a nonthreatening adult I could say: Well, if you aren't angry, what would you say you are feeling now?"

"Just annoyed." When I asked him to describe what

that felt like, he reported feelings usually associated with anger. I then was able to sensitize him to times when he was "annoyed" so he could understand his anger better. A good deal was accomplished by avoiding arguing with him when he retreated into the parent role.

MENTORING LESSON 33: *When you feel an emotional reaction in yourself, try to move to an adult role rather than being hooked into playing a child or parent role. And help others to do the same.*

⌒

The Soil of Passion

NOT ONLY MUST mentors help people to maintain perspective in interpersonal encounters but they must also encourage them to keep a sense of balance in their lives so they feel strong enough to withstand interpersonal pressures. However, this is difficult because of the great range of personalities and lifestyles.

Over the past twenty years working with professional helpers and healers, I have learned that the amount of activity or responsibility is not the key factor in the stress people experience in their vocations. Instead, it is an array of elements such as sense of being in control, satisfaction, willingness to fail, and time to renew oneself.

This last factor is especially important in today's stressful world. Time to relax, unwind, gain perspective, absorb loss, create alternatives, and enjoy one's world is one of the strongest antidotes to imbalance. And this renewal can be done in little ways that have the potential for dramatic benefit.

My own schedule is incredibly full. As well as being chairperson of a series of graduate programs with over three hundred students, I teach graduate courses, am a consultant, lecture internationally and nationally, write, mentor several people, and am married. Yet I find carving out an hour for a walk or taking the time to relax, garden, or make a refreshing call to a friend lets me keep balanced during my usually busy days. It also leaves me rested and nourished enough to be fully present to those I serve and open to help others in times of crisis.

People ask me if such little restbits are enough. I say, "Of course not, but I must be very faithful to them, because my neighbors told me they thought I retired a few years ago and the UPS delivery man greeted me last week with the exclamation `You home again? Don't you have a job?' " (Snarky fellow, no tip for him!)

We have to do what we can to keep balanced given the realities of our lives. Otherwise, we will lose our energy and passion for life. It doesn't take much to bring the level of stress down a peg, to where we feel challenged but not harried, involved but not preoccupied, engaged but not put upon by others.

Spending a few moments of quiet in the morning, taking a coffee or walking break wherever it can be fit in, having some time in the car listening to music or National

Public Radio, making a phone call to a friend, reading a good book, and seeing a movie while enjoying some popcorn are things we can do daily or weekly. Time in the park on the weekend and a visit with friends—at least monthly—will also help us drop our stress and realize how precious life is.

There is a proverb that says: "Life is something that happens while we are busy doing something else." How sad it is not to be present for your own life but to be caught in a mental envelope of worries while racing to your death.

Even when I have a day of what appears to be seamless work, I break it up with thirty seconds of deep breathing, a walk down the hall while recalling loving faces, or a funny story shared with a colleague. My life is too challenging not to do this. My life is too precious to believe I'm letting others down if I do. And in this style of balanced living and willingness to get quickly back on course when I lose perspective, I am modeling one of the greatest lessons I can for those I mentor.

MENTORING LESSON 34: *Make a serious commitment to maintain your balance and renew your passion by breaking up the day with a walk, a cup of tea or coffee, a phone call, or a chat with a friend. And take time weekly or monthly to be in touch with nature, go to the movies, visit a friend, or otherwise refresh yourself.*

35. STOPPING

Flow, Don't Drift

A BALANCED LIFE is one in which we flow, don't drift, through our days, weeks, and years. At points in life roadblocks appear to derail this natural movement. Small things such as a pulled leg muscle, a restless night, or a forgotten wallet or more major events such as cancer, a divorce, or a serious financial loss can turn a graceful life into something difficult. But, does this need to be so?

What if these blocks, unpleasant or terrible though they are, were also seen as stops in the road to remind us that we are not paying attention to what is important: our familiar surroundings, our inner, spiritual life, or our chance to absorb wisdom.

Tibetan Buddhists often decry the Western style of life that says running through each day to earn money, power, fame, or success is practical. But many Americans and Europeans see attending to dharma (spiritual practice), which will in fact help us appreciate life's many gifts, as foolish and unattainable.

It's obvious that obstacles, unpleasant news, and negative events are unwanted. Yet if we fail to use them as wake-up calls to better appreciate our lives, we are being wasteful. Moreover, we will not be able to help those who come to us for mentoring appreciate the same opportunities amid the sad events in their lives.

MENTORING LESSON 35: *Use negative events as reminders to stop and appreciate life's gifts.*

⌒

What Is...Is Wonderful!

MENTORING OTHERS OFTEN demonstrates "parallel process." As we relate with the people who seek mentoring from us, they learn to treat others whom they guide in a similar way. People often learn more from what we model and how we act than from what we say.

Consequently, the heart of our attitude toward those seeking mentoring should be acceptance. If we can truly accept the people coming to us, then almost magical results are possible. First, people will be willing to share almost anything and look at their faults or defenses more freely. If people feel valued, they trust that their faults or foibles won't harm the relationship. Second, people who feel accepted tend to have enough self-esteem to reach out and offer others unconditional acceptance.

Accepting others is simple and profound but sometimes not easy. Two steps make the process more possible.

One, because accepting others is easier when we feel at ease with ourselves, take time each morning to quietly center yourself on the deep conviction *I am loved*. You can nourish this belief by remembering those who care for you and visualizing their smiling, encouraging faces. If no one comes to mind now, remember good people at previous stages of your life. For those who are religious, visualizing a loving God with whom you are in covenant (lasting relationship) will help as well.

Two, make an effort to seed a positive attitude toward others. You can foster this attitude of true hospitality by recalling that the person seeking mentoring was once a little child cuddled and loved by parents or guardians. Getting in touch with the child present in the adult helps to be open to someone who is now a grouchy grown-up. Mentally, try to soothe the irritable, colicky child who is now facing you as an older person. Also, seek to quickly uncover a person's talents.

These talents, once noted and shared, aid in mutual recognition of the goodness present in the individual. In addition, such talents offer a gold mine of knowledge to increase self-awareness, which will grow if the person in mentoring feels accepted. For example, talents often become liabilities when people get anxious (a leader with initiative can become dominant if not sensitive to other people). In addition, talents are helpful in diagnosing with whom and under what circumstances a person gets defensive.

MENTORING LESSON 36: *Accept yourself by getting in touch with self-love and the love you receive from others. Then take that self-acceptance into mentoring by accepting the people coming to see you.*

37. Summarizing

You Don't Need to Confront

People who are mentors often ask me: "What is the best way to confront those I am asked to guide?" My answer, which usually surprises them, is: "Don't confront. Instead, summarize what the person has told you about the situation, the information itself will confront." For instance, each time people use a certain style they annoy others, by citing several illustrations and summarizing in a way they can see clearly, you can lead them to see the pattern for themselves and decide whether they want to continue this behavior.

People tend to be especially defensive when they see foibles or failures that are part of their overall style of dealing with the world. They feel, "If this style is a problem, then I am a problem." Also, stress is produced by not knowing or feeling comfortable with other styles of interacting, managing, or pursuing goals.

Consequently, I usually point out the talents people have that are akin to the problems they are experiencing. This approach gives them the message that the core of their personality and relating style need not change. On the contrary, if they can see when and why their talents become exaggerated and don't work, they can modify these talents in a way that will make them more effective.

For instance, if a man is passionate and inspirational in the way he presents material to individuals and groups, this is a wonderful talent to use in a measured way so its effect is not wasted. However, if this same man dominates conversations when he feels anxious and insecure, he needs to know this. Otherwise, his gift of motivating people may turn people off.

MENTORING LESSON 37: *Instead of confronting people, summarize what they have told you so the information itself confronts them and encourages them to modify their talents.*

~

Primitive Pouting

SOMETIMES PEOPLE BEHAVE as if they were two, three, or four years of age. If effect, they are saying: "I didn't get what I needed at this age, and I refuse to grow up until someone meets these needs and convinces me all will be fine forever." These blocks in certain areas are common even in the healthiest of people. But awareness of their presence helps people understand why others react negatively to them. So, if you notice, for instance, that people tend to talk on and on when they don't feel heard it is good to bring this unhelpful style of behavior to the person's attention.

Mentoring, of course, is not psychotherapy. You are not there to work through unrealistic transferences, uncover unconscious conflicts, or attempt personality change. However, when a person is behaving like a child, some questioning about the behavior can be very helpful. Tone of voice, impulsivity, unrealistic expectations, and other seemingly childish styles need to be described so people can chose between continuing this behavior and striving for more mature interactions.

MENTORING LESSON 38: *Make people aware of when their behavior seems uncharacteristically childish so they can see what needs they are holding on to in a way that interferes with mature interactions.*

39. JOURNALING

Keeping Heart Notes

MENTORING IS REALLY helpful when those persons seeking it bring in not only specific events but also their feelings about the events when they happened. To make this possible, I ask people to consider daily journaling.

The process is quite simple. Just take a little spiral notebook and spend a few moments at the end of the day jotting down some reflections. They need not be in careful prose; even complete sentences are not necessary.

By running through the day mentally like a newsreel, we can relive the highlights. Then, by noting any events that carry emotion—either positive or negative—as well as any questions, confusions, beliefs or thoughts about them, we can come to see the meaning in the incidents. Further, the journal's perceptions, perspectives, and conclusions are there to be reviewed.

Journaling makes it easier to observe ourselves, our tendencies in behavior, and life's paradoxes. Also, it gives this person practice getting in touch with deep feelings about others, change or loss, and what sparks emotions. Values and catalysts for shifts in inner balance or perspective also can come to the fore when we journal. Journaling as a means of enhancing self-awareness can be a very beneficial practice for mentors as well as the people who seek mentoring.

MENTORING LESSON 39: *Encourage people to journal so tendencies, values, feelings, and confusions can become more evident.*

Koans

Koan IS THE JAPANESE word for a puzzle life presents us with. Koans come in all forms: As a teacher, should I spend time helping an inexperienced colleague if it means depriving my own class of attention? As a minister, can I suggest people pray if I've given up praying myself? As an A.A. sponsor, should I continue working with someone I've grown to dislike if she or he doesn't know it and has been rejected by others? As a supervisor, am I bound to tell people I'm mentoring that I'm angry if they don't seem to follow my guidance but show up for each session promptly and listen intently to my feedback?

Of course, there is no one ideal answer to any koan. Yet how we "solve" these riddles determines whether we move forward in life. To progress, one must shift a way of thinking or believing that is stagnant. The more a person is caught in a frame of reference or set of rules, the less change or an innovative freeing response to a koan is possible. Perhaps the most critical koan we face in life is, "Who am I really?" Through the mentoring relationship, we explore ways to gain sufficient freedom and inner ease to be who we really are so that we, in turn, can be a helping presence to others.

This is why in mentoring, rather than provide solutions, we gently ask: What if? What's the worst thing that would happen if you did ___? Mentoring, in essence, is helping people question everything so they can chart their own course. Mentoring doesn't provide answers. It provides the setting in which people reframe both questions and answers for themselves.

MENTORING LESSON 40: *In essence, mentoring helps people reframe for themselves both the questions (koans) in their lives and the answers.*

Inner Ease—Mentoring Others, Mentoring Self

INNER EASE: *A state of interior freedom resulting from a relaxed, honest appreciation of one's ordinary self, which spontaneously results in sharing oneself with others in a way that encourages the best in them as well.*

WHEN WE ARE in the presence of someone who possesses inner ease, we may find ourselves peacefully flowing with the universe as well. We might wonder, Why can't I be like this all the time? Sadly, most of us don't go beyond wistfully asking this question. This book is for the few who do because the essence of mentoring is experiencing inner ease and then sharing this gentle place with others.

As a mentor my overall goal is to help people achieve

their own inner ease. To live a relaxed and meaningful life and be in a position eventually to mentor others, people have to find out who they are, value themselves, and live out of that identity in a secure and spontaneous way.

Before we reach this awareness, so much energy is wasted on defensiveness that little is left for creativity, growth... simply living! It is easy to be lured by advertising and the influences of society and family to be someone other than who we are meant to be. The message we often hear is: Your ordinary selves are not enough. To deal with this, an informal education on how to better appreciate who we are and share it with others becomes part of the mentoring process.

Meeting a person who is at ease with the true self is a healing experience. People who are at ease are without guile, transparent, and free. The wind of what is really good seems to blow through them so we are refreshed by it as well. When we are with such people, we feel the courage to let down our defenses until in no time at all it takes no courage to face, and simply be, our ordinary selves.

This experience may occur when we are in a therapy, mentoring, or spiritual guidance relationship. We also may encounter it with a true friend. Such a meeting sets the stage for a generous and true relationship with ourselves. So ordinariness—recognizing and appreciating the core genuine self as well as challenging whatever is luring us to hide, puff up, or debase ourselves—is the fruit of meetings with people of goodwill. And greater freedom is the overall result.

What if we could be mentors like this not just to others but also to ourselves on a daily basis? What if we set the stage for inner ease by being gentle and clear in how we view ourselves? What if we saw ordinariness, our own uniqueness, as something of value and lived out our lives accordingly? Wouldn't it be worth the effort?

If we have a map and clear directions to where we are traveling, isn't the trip more enjoyable? Wouldn't the same be the case with our own life's journey?

Reflect on these words of the accomplished inventor Buckminster Fuller:

> The only important thing about me is that I am an average, healthy human being. All the things I've been able to do, any human being, or any one, or you, could do equally well or better. I was able to accomplish what I did by refusing to be hooked on a game of life that had nothing to do with the way the universe was going.

Think about these words from the poet e. e. cummings as well:

> To be nobody but yourself in a world which is doing its best, night and day, to make you everybody else—means to fight the hardest battle any human being can fight, and never stop fighting.

And see if you agree with the lesson in this little story from the theologian Martin Buber:

The Rabbi Zusya said a short time before his death, "In the world to come, I shall not be asked, 'Why were you not Moses?' Instead, I shall be asked, 'Why were you not Zusya?' "

To be a good friend to yourself as well as to others, you must be willing to take the time to be gentle, honest, and hopeful. You need to have the courage to value yourself and to live your life accordingly. You must also see your life as a work of art to be respected, fathomed, and, of course, generously—but not compulsively—shared.

All these aspects are part and parcel of a psychologically and spiritually healthy life. Take a few moments to think about them. Reflect on how they are part of your attitude toward yourself and life. If they are not present, why? If they are present, how can they be reinforced? Now look back through the table of contents, find a chapter title that particularly intrigues you, and start there. Following this, choose another topic, and so on until you have reread this book. All this reading and reflection will encourage and enhance your sense of inner ease and help you integrate the mentoring principles in a deeper way.

We must learn to relax with and ultimately discover the true self through many avenues. Whatever is valuable must be brought to bear. If a mentor used only one approach with every person, it would be like a surgeon recommending an appendectomy for everyone who came to the office. Obviously, this single mindedness would achieve uneven medical results. So you will find some of the topics in this book more relevant than others. This is natural. However, don't set aside too quickly a review of the other chapters. They may address issues and agendas that you are not familiar with but that are still important for you.

Once you have finished reviewing the chapters of this book and spent some time with Appendixes I and II, you can consult Appendix III for additional reading to help you continue the mentoring process. Also, I suggest that you start an informal journal in which you can jot down daily reflections. First use it to note your responses to the questions and discussions in the book; then use it to note observations about yourself and your interactions during the day, especially instances of providing or receiving informal mentoring. That is what the chapters in this book are: my own reflections as a result of my work with others and myself. Journaling is simple, quick, and quite useful in mapping your life's journey so you don't lose your way for long.

The material in this book is provided in the belief that you have many possibilities within you that you can open up and share with others. You need only encouragement and structure to do so.

I wish you the best in both receiving and imparting
life's wisdom because

Having a mentor to help us
find who we are meant to be
is a worthwhile undertaking.
Sharing the person we have found
within ourselves freely with others
is an honorable way to live.
And, doing both with a sense of freedom,
is truly an invitation to live with a refreshing spirit
...of *inner ease*.

Answers to Common Questions on Mentoring

How is mentoring different from psychotherapy, counseling, or spiritual direction or discipleship?

Mentoring often looks like these processes, but it differs in focus. Psychotherapy deals with psychological (emotional, functional) difficulties, counseling is issue-oriented, and spiritual direction or discipleship focuses on one's relationship with God. Mentoring is noteworthy for its breadth. Its concern is one's overall decisions with respect to work, family, relationships, and finding life's meaning given one's own values and belief system. In essence, the goal of mentoring is clarity and the approach is collaboration.

Who is able to do mentoring?

All adults are called to be mentors although the types of people being guided will be dictated by the situation. For instance, parents obviously have a natural opportunity for mentoring their children, as do supervisors for mentoring the people who work for them. Sponsors in A.A. are also in a good position to mentor those in recovery.

How is mentoring initiated?

Generally, there are three ways to establish a mentoring relationship. The best is when the individual who wants mentoring takes responsibility for setting up the process. Another common way is when the relationship dictates it, for example a supervisor on the job, a parent with a child, or someone who by virtue of his or her vocation (clergy, physician, teacher) is expected to offer mentoring as part of the role being filled. The least desirable is when a person offers mentoring without being asked or being in a role that includes giving guidance. However, this is not to say that mentoring shouldn't be offered. Initiating a mentoring relationship with someone who might benefit from our guidance can be a true act of generosity.

What are the downsides or dangers in offering mentoring to someone who hasn't asked for it?

There are five possible downsides to offering mentoring when someone hasn't asked for it:

1. You may be being intrusive.
2. You may be acting more out of your desire to help than her or his need to have you as a mentor.

3. The chemistry may not be right between you.
4. You may cause a person who is unable to set limits to say yes when he or she really feels no.
5. You may be unaware that you have a hidden agenda, which will undercut your ability to be open to the person's own desires and goals.

So what's the best way to see if I could be of help in cases where I really believe I can offer needed support?

Be tentative in your offer. Indicate that you wonder if it would be helpful if you sat down with a person periodically to be a sounding board and offer some feedback. Suggest that the person think about it (even if the answer was yes) and let you know if, after a bit of reflection, he or she sees your offer as useful.

How do I find a mentor?

Look at the people in your life now that you respect. It is easiest to approach someone who already knows you and with whom you have some experience—even if it has been quite informal. You can also ask friends, relatives or colleagues for recommendations. If there is no potential mentor in your immediate circle, seeking someone you don't know is the logical next step. You can ask someone to meet with you briefly to discuss a personal or professional concern in person, over the phone, or via the mail or E-mail.

Should I expect to pay for mentoring?

Most informal mentoring is done without charge. Formal mentoring (teachers, business supervisors, and so on) may either be funded by the organization or be done gratis. Mentoring is different from therapy, counseling, and clinical supervision which usually have fees, and spiritual direction for which a donation is often given. Although there are some exceptions (when the mentor requires the income for support), my personal view is that mentoring should be offered without cost—as it has been by elders for those seeking their guidance through the ages.

How often should we meet?

Frequency of meeting depends on the situation. In the case of business or teaching mentorship it may be weekly, with an A.A. sponsor it may be more or less frequent according to need. Outside these specific situations, though, meetings are generally not more frequent than every other week, with the norm being every four to six weeks. These guidelines are important for those who are not professional helpers, so that the relationship does not become too intense for the average person to understand and handle.

If I am offering or receiving mentoring and the relationship doesn't seem helpful or appropriate, what should I do?

The first step is to discuss your concern with the other

person. Discussing what is happening in the mentoring relationship with another person wiser than yourself is also a good idea.

How should we structure our meetings to make the most use of our time together?

Usually a minute or so is spent in greeting. Then a simple question such as "How are things going?" is a good opening. If the response is very concise ("Fine"), either silence or a further prompt ("I'm glad things are fine. Put me in the picture by describing for me what's going well") should enable the person seeking mentoring to begin speaking at greater length. Following this, reflection, summarization, and additional questions will help the person gain greater clarity. Finally, a few minutes before your time is up, provide a short wrap-up and schedule your next time together. The total timeframe for each meeting is usually forty-five to sixty minutes.

Is there a simple approach to becoming a good mentor?

Yes, I think there is. Being a good mentor involves a balance between structure and spontaneity as well as the willingness to put a little effort into learning and practicing certain lessons.

The structure in mentoring is simple. Most people already practice it at times. Basically, mentoring is a purposeful conversation that offers a safe, supportive place to tell one's story, achieve greater clarity, solve a problem, and get feedback from a more experienced, wiser colleague, friend, or family member.

To accomplish this, simply use your own talents to welcome, draw out, respond to, support, and sometimes challenge those who seek your listening ear. With this in mind, you need only be yourself, because your style, as well as your wisdom, is what probably attracted the person seeking mentoring to you.

The lessons in this book are designed to make the mentoring relationship richer. By concentrating on one lesson in each mentoring session, you can get better and better at placing your own natural talents at the service of the person being mentored.

If mentoring is effective, what changes?

Effective mentoring increases knowledge and changes attitude. Of these two, the attitude is the more important. Mentoring should lead to greater inner freedom, less grasping, more gratitude, and the joining of humility with knowledge that is known as wisdom.

The person seeking mentoring should also become more sincere and transparent—if not with others, at least with himself or herself and the mentor. This is essential if a person is to fully appreciate both talents and growing edges. Without honesty, growth is very difficult and true depth is practically impossible.

Since mentoring, growth, and change are all good things, why would someone resist such progress?

Usually the source of resistance is anxiety about seeing the truth about oneself and one's situation. People are worried that if they see themselves and things as they really are, their comfort will be disturbed. More specifically, people are afraid they will see things they don't like about themselves or recognize that they have wasted part of their lives. Also, they are concerned that insight will require them to change—not only in ways that may be difficult for them but also in ways that may produce negative reactions from others who are used to them behaving as they have in the past.

How is this resistance to change overcome?

First, the discomfort of staying the same encourages people who want to take the risk to change. Also, people usually take heart from their mentors. They feel that the mentors seem to have derived benefit from change and growth so they will too. Finally, by making changes in increments, people are usually able to see that while initially there may be some discomfort, in the end the truth and healthy change will indeed set them free.

Who determines the areas and extent of change?

Always it is the person seeking mentoring who dictates the areas and extent of change. Mentors have to be careful not to impose their agendas on others. That is why period-ically discerning goals in mentoring is a good idea.

When I feel lost in the mentoring process, what should I do or say?

You can do two things when you start to feel lost in the mentoring process. First, recall to yourself the goals that brought you together in the first place. Then ask the person you are mentoring where he or she feels you are going relative to your original goals.

—

If you have questions on the mentoring process, please feel free to send them to me (Dr. Robert J. Wicks, Loyola College, Suite 302, 7135 Minstrel Way, Columbia, MD 21045 or via E-mail at rwicks@loyola.edu) and I will try to address them in subsequent editions of this book.

~

Summary of Mentoring Lessons

1. Make your mentoring relationships safe enough for people to share intense feelings.

2. Use respect as the litmus test in seeking or providing mentorship.

3. Offer a receptive listening-space where people can tell their stories.

4. Be sure you don't stop exploring issues too soon; question further, asking for illustrations and clear examples.

5. Encourage people not merely to speak about changing or progressing but focus on role models who can be emulated in little ways each day.

6. Urge people to take responsibility for their behavior and to become more aware of the consequences of each of their actions.

7. When people feel upset over a failure or an onslaught on their image, invite them to laugh at themselves.

8. Help people foster gratefulness by recognizing the many people and things—including their own talents—that they should appreciate and enjoy.

9. Ask people to reflect on what one word would best describe them. Then encourage them to find a second word to modify or "buff" the first so their presence to others is more balanced.

10. To cultivate a growthful and open mentoring process, foster intrigue about people's behavior—both successes and failures—and excitement about the process of discovery that leads to clarity.

11. Show people how to utilize a negative interpersonal encounter by experiencing it fully, then letting their feelings flow away from the experience, and finally, looking at the encounter objectively.

12. In every situation help people look carefully for what is within their control.

13. When you feel overwhelmed by a story or question put to you, follow these four steps: (1) Take note of your feelings. (2) Tell yourself you don't have to have the one perfect answer or an "instant cure." (3) Let the person know you recognize he or she must be feeling overwhelmed. (4) Ask questions that allow the problem to be addressed in a manageable, logical way.

14. Show that you value your relationships with those you are mentoring in little ways, such as being prompt, attentive, and responsive about what they are sharing and how they are progressing.

15. In supporting people to become clear about what they want, help them see that they might have to let go of something else that may be equally desirable.

16. Recognize that some problems have developed over years. Don't be discouraged by this, but let it encourage hope, patience, and an appreciation of step-by-step solutions.

17. Be fully yourself (a passionate presence), and be practical—listen carefully, help seek greater clarity, and share your own wisdom and experience.

18. Encourage people to spend time daily in silence and solitude—even if it's only two or three minutes—to integrate the lessons of mentoring and of life.

19. Help people bring to the surface, examine, and discard hidden rules that limit their freedom and are no longer relevant to their lives.

20. Use your experience to help educate people in ways of approaching life differently. Offer them fresh information and advice that will be helpful in their particular, unique situation.

21. After experiencing someone's strong emotions, take a step back and offer this logical problem-solving approach: ventilation, diagnosis, planning, intervention, and letting go.

22. Help people turn negative experiences into life lessons by experiencing them fully, understanding them completely, and letting them go.

23. Model and teach patience as a way to let people and systems heal themselves. When dealing with difficult people, have low expectations and high hopes.

24. Value who you are as an ordinary person and see life as truly precious; then your passionate, courageous attitude will be positively infectious.

25. Be attuned to your feelings so you can recognize when your own denials, repressions, or interpersonal games come to light in a mentoring interaction. And model being open to helpful albeit unpleasant insight.

26. Notice the essential learning that is present in all failures and losses so it can be integrated into people's wisdom.

27. When people relate profound spiritual or psychological experiences, help them explore the fruits of these events.

28. Maintain a reasonable distance from the negativity of others and maintain perspective through morning meditation focused on the preciousness and brevity of life. Also, keep a sense of humor handy to break the negative projections people try to place on you.

29. Accept your responsibility for maintaining boundaries. Being surprised is no excuse for failure to honor boundaries.

30. Remind yourself and others to use the red flag of annoyance to see the need to withdraw projections and let peace, composure, and gratitude return.

31. Take a few minutes in silence and solitude each evening to review your day nonjudgmentally so you can get closure and learn how to help others do the same.

32. Once you have listened to people's concerns, explore what they did and how effective it was; seek as much clarity as possible, offer as many helpful responses as you can, then let the outcome rest lightly.

33. When you feel an emotional reaction in yourself, try to move to an adult role rather than being hooked into playing a child or parent role. And help others to do the same.

34. Make a serious commitment to maintain your balance and renew your passion by breaking up the day with a walk, a cup of tea or coffee, a phone call, or a chat with a friend. And take time weekly or monthly to be in nature, go to the movies, visit a friend, or otherwise refresh yourself.

35. Use negative events as reminders to stop and appreciate life's gifts.

36. Accept yourself by getting in touch with self-love and the love you receive from others. Then take that self-acceptance into mentoring by accepting the people coming to see you.

37. Instead of confronting people, summarize what they have told you so the information itself confronts them and encourages them to modify their talents.

38. Make people aware of when their behavior seems uncharacteristically childish so they can see what needs they are holding on to in a way that interferes with mature interactions.

39. Encourage people to journal so tendencies, values, feelings, and confusions can become more evident.

40. In essence, mentoring helps people reframe for themselves both the questions (koans) in their lives and the answers.

~

Readings to Enrich the Mentoring Process: An Annotated Bibliography

IF THIS MENTORING primer has whet your appetite, as I hope it has, the following readings can further enrich the process. My only proviso is that as you read them you keep this book's structure and lessons on mentoring in mind. Doing so is essential to avoid drifting into being a therapist or spiritual director.

Among my own books, two can help improve your overall mentoring skills. I think the best work I've written to date is *Living a Gentle, Passionate Life* (Paulist Press, 1998). It offers a simple "country psychology" and a broad spirituality as ways of nurturing one's inner life. This framework will help you to gain perspective and frame questions and offer guidelines when people seem lost or lack balance.

The other book of my own I would suggest is *Companions in Hope* (Paulist Press, 1998). Originally published with Chilton, it has been updated and expanded by Thomas Rodgerson, a colleague of mine who also added a pastoral dimension so it would be not only useful to anyone wishing basic listening–counseling skills but also relevant to people interested in a faith dimension. Whether you are religious or not, this book will give you sound information on topics such as questioning, clarifying, and caring. There is also a section on referral for professional help, which is important when you recognize that a person's difficulties require more than mentoring.

Books that offer interactions between wisdom figures and their disciples can also provide insight into the spirit and potential depth of the mentoring process. Among many good books of this kind are Rainer Maria Rilke's *Letters to a Young Poet* (Norton, 1954), Andrew Harvey's *Journey in Ladakh* (Houghton Mifflin, 1983), Sandy Johnson's *Book of Tibetan Elders* (Riverhead Books, 1996), Henri Nouwen's *Genesee Diary* (Doubleday, Image, 1981), Anthony de Mello's *One Minute Wisdom* (Doubleday, 1985) and David Chadwick's *Crooked Cucumber: The Life and Zen Teaching of Shunryu Suzuki* (Broadway Books, 1999). Also, the very popular *Tuesdays with Morrie* (Doubleday, 1997) by Mitch Albom provides a good example of the spirit of mentoring.

Books of quotations also can seed a sound mentoring spirit. One of my favorites is *The Last Word: A Treasury of Women's Quotes* (Prentice Hall, 1992), edited by Carolyn Warner. There are many more collections that offer insight into a broad range of thinkers and topics that reveal experiences beyond the confines of our sometimes parochial lives.

Biographies and autobiographies can do this too. In my book *After 50* (Paulist Press, 1997), I wrote

In the introduction to the Radcliffe Biography Series, Matina S. Horner writes: "Fine biographies give us both a glimpse of ourselves and a reflection of the human spirit. Biography illuminates history, inspires by example, and fires the imagination to life's possibilities. Good biography can create life-long models for us. Reading about other people's experiences encourages us to persist, to face hardship, and to feel less alone. Biography tells us about choice, the power of a personal vision, and the interdependence of human life."

Reading contemporary autobiographies such as Maya Angelou's *I Know Why the Caged Bird Sings* (Bantam Books, 1971), Etty Hillesum's *An Interrupted Life* (Pocket Books, 1985), the Dalai Lama's *Freedom in Exile* (*Harper* Collins, 1991), or

Thomas Merton's *Seven Storey Mountain* (Harcourt Brace and Jovanovich, 1948), all bear out Dr. Horner's comments. Also, reading biographies such as Robert Cole's *Dorothy Day: A Radical Devotion* (Addison-Wesley, 1987) or A. N. Wilson's life of C.S. Lewis (Norton, 1990) brings us into the world of persons who can help us see life differently than we might, given our own limited background. The possibilities of both autobiographies and biographies, contemporary and classic, are often overlooked by many of us for more "attractive, exciting reading." Once exposed to this type of book, though, we begin to see that real adventure is entering deeply into the life of another—especially one who faced the despair of life and didn't give in to the situation. (p. 54)

Basic books on interviewing, listening, and human relationships can also be helpful. By reviewing what is available in the self-help and psychology/psychiatry sections of your local bookstore, you can continually find books to nourish and improve your mentoring skills and ability to make use of the wisdom that is all around you if you are simply open enough to see it.

Finally, what I refer to as "journey books," in which people share their views of life's challenges, rewards, and perils, are helpful. Four such books that come to mind are

Richard Bode's *First You Have to Row a Little Boat* (Warner Books, 1993), Sue Bender's *Plain and Simple* (Harper & Row, 1989), Annie Dillard's *The Writing Life* (Harper & Row, 1989), and Doris Grumbach's *Fifty Days of Solitude* (Beacon Press, 1994).

To really appreciate the wisdom contained in such books and be able to share their concepts and life lessons in your mentoring, a good deal of effort is needed. To my mind, reading less and absorbing more is better than skimming through a wide range of volumes and remembering little.

Intentional reading requires an eye to uncovering sutras (brief aphorisms), which you can use to guide your own life as well as the lives of those who come to you for mentoring. Once you have spotted such essential statements, underline them in the text, then copy them out for further reflection and study. The ones that turn out to really resonate with your philosophy of living, you should seek to learn and overlearn until you have absorbed them into your way of looking at, and living, life. Only then will there be a difference...and what a wonderful difference it will be!